Women in Space

By N. B. Grace

The Child's World®
www.childsworld.com

Published in the United States of America by The Child's World®
P.O. Box 326 • Chanhassen, MN 55317-0326
800-599-READ • www.childsworld.com

This book is for my father, a NASA engineer who always told me to aim for the stars! —N.B.G.

ACKNOWLEDGMENTS

The Child's World®: Mary Berendes, Publishing Director

Produced by Shoreline Publishing Group LLC
President / Editorial Director: James Buckley, Jr.
Designer: Tom Carling, carlingdesign.com
Cover Art: Slimfilms
Copy Editor: Beth Adelman

Photo Credits
Cover—Main image: SlimFilms; astronauts: AP/Wide World
Interior—AP/Wide World: 9, 12, 24, 29; Corbis: 5;
Getty Images: 6, 8, 11, 15, 17, 26; Courtesy NASA: 18, 21, 25, 27;
iStock: 7; Photos.com: 23.

LIBRARY OF CONGRESS CATALOGING-IN-PUBLICATION DATA

Grace, N. B.
  Women in space / by N.B. Grace.
    p. cm. — (Girls rock!)
  Includes bibliographical references and index.
  ISBN 1-59296-751-5 (library bound : alk. paper)
 1. Women astronauts—United States—Juvenile literature. 2. Women astronauts—Soviet Union—Biography—Juvenile literature. 3. Astronautics—United States—History—Juvenile literature. 4. Astronautics—Soviet Union—History—Juvenile literature. I. Title. II. Series.
  TL789.85.A1G73 2006
  629.450092'2—dc22
                        2006001645

CONTENTS

THE Pioneers

People have probably always wondered what it would be like to zoom up from the earth and fly toward the stars. In the 1960s, that dream started to become a reality. In 1961, Yuri Gagarin, a **cosmonaut** from the Soviet Union, was the first person to fly into space. Shortly after that, two American astronauts each made one trip into space but didn't enter **orbit**. In 1962, John Glenn became the

first American to orbit the earth, circling it three times. Longer space flights followed. In 1969, Neil Armstrong became the first person to walk on the moon! These space travel pioneers happen to be men—but women have played an important part of space exploration, too!

Cosmonaut Valentina Tereshkova models the helmet she wore during her historic 1963 flight.

When Valentina Tereshkova (TEHR-esh-KAW-vuh) was growing up in the Soviet Union, she loved adventure. While taking her college classes by mail, she took up parachuting. She made 126

jumps before she was 26. She also worked to fulfill her dream of flying in space.

In 1961, she wrote to her government to ask if women could become cosmonauts. The answer was yes. After passing the same tests male cosmonauts took, she joined the Soviet space team.

Back in the USSR

Valentina grew up in the Union of Soviet Socialist Republics (USSR), also called the Soviet Union. In 1991, this huge country split up into one large nation and many smaller ones. Today, the large nation is called Russia.

On June 16, 1963, the Soviets launched a rocket carrying *Vostok 6*, a space **capsule** with Valentina on board. She orbited the Earth for 70 hours. She was the first woman in space!

When she returned safely from space, Valentina received many honors from her country.

After her flight, Valentina became famous in the Soviet Union and inspired thousands of girls. In 1969, she earned her college degree after years of taking classes by mail.

In 2003, on the 40th anniversary of her flight, Valentina was honored again. She is still a national hero.

Other female cosmonauts made space history as space exploration continued. In 1982, cosmonaut Svetlana Savitskaya (SAV-it-SKY-ah) became the first woman to make a **spacewalk**.

When America's space program first started, the United States and the Soviet Union were both trying to be the first country to send someone into space. In 1959, the U.S. tested 31 men to see whether they had the skills to become American astronauts. Seven men, the Mercury 7, were chosen to be astronauts in the new Mercury program.

Mercury was the name of an ancient Greek god. He was the god of speed and brought messages from the gods to humans.

What most people didn't know, however, is that 19 women took the same tests! These tests lasted for weeks and were extremely hard. The men and women who wanted to become astronauts had every part of their bodies tested to see if they could survive in space.

The Mercury 7 are shown here trying on their silver space suits.

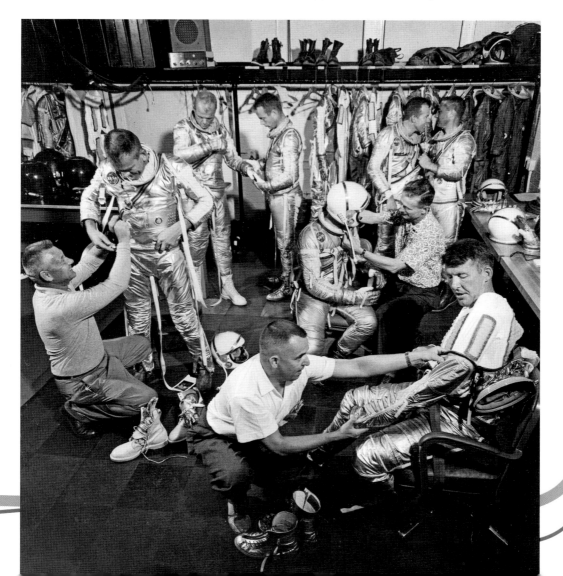

Record-setting pilot Jerrie Cobb was one of the women who trained to become a Mercury astronaut. A pilot since her high-school days, she flew just about every type of airplane. After being kept out of the astronaut program, Jerrie used her flying skills to help others, especially people living in the Amazon River jungle.

In the end, 13 women—the Mercury 13—passed all the tests. However, the American government wasn't really ready for the idea of sending women into space. Instead, the government ended the program. None of the Mercury 13 women got to become astronauts.

The Mercury 13 women didn't have the chance to go into space, but they led the way for women to follow. American women would end up in space—although it took another 23 years!

What sorts of women tried out to be astronauts? All were pilots, but some were also scientists, teachers, or were in the military.

2

U.S. WOMEN IN Space

By the time Sally Ride was 14, she was a star tennis player. In elementary school and junior high school, she also studied math and science. Even then, she was always interested in space.

Sally studied **astrophysics** at Stanford University in California. One day, she saw an ad—NASA was looking for people who wanted to be astronauts!

Sally applied for the job—but so did 8,000 other people! After going through testing and meeting with NASA officials, Sally got her wish. In 1978, NASA selected her to be an astronaut.

Sally Ride poses for her first photo as a member of NASA's astronaut program in 1978.

The space shuttle was a new type of spacecraft that first flew in 1981. The shuttle was the first space vehicle that could be used again and again.

At NASA, Sally trained to be an astronaut and designed gear for the new space shuttle. She also worked in **Mission Control** during the 1982 flight of the space shuttle *Columbia*. She was the first woman in Mission Control to talk to astronauts during a flight.

Then, in 1983, Sally made history. She flew into space as a **mission specialist** on the *Challenger* space shuttle. She became the first American woman in space. At age 32, she was also the

On the space shuttle, Sally helped do experiments to learn more about space.

youngest American astronaut to orbit the Earth.

"All adventures, especially into new territory, are scary," Sally said. But she was willing to take the risk!

The metal ring at the top of Eileen Collins' spacesuit is used to attach a helmet that helps her breathe in space.

Sally Ride made her mark as the first American woman in space, but no woman had ever **piloted** a spacecraft—until Eileen Collins. Even as a child growing up in Elmira, New York, Eileen loved airplanes. Her father took her to the local airport to watch airplanes. When Eileen was in college, she worked part-time to earn money for flying lessons.

Her love of flight led her to the U.S. Air Force Academy. There she became an outstanding pilot.

Learning to Fly

The U.S. Air Force Academy is in Colorado Springs, Colorado. It's like a regular college, except that all the students are members of the United States Air Force. Many study to become pilots.

Eileen became the first woman to pilot a space shuttle when she flew *Discovery* on a mission in 1995. She flew another shuttle mission in 1997. She was the pilot and NASA's first woman **commander** on two more missions in 1999 and 2005.

"Some people might look at the things I've done in my life—flying jets or flying the space shuttle—and say that I'm a risk taker," Eileen said. "I think that really makes my life an adventure."

3

TRAGEDY AND Triumph

Since space travel began, everyone involved with space flights has worked hard to make them as safe as possible. Even so, accidents happen.

The U.S. space program has had several terrible accidents. One of the worst happened on January 28, 1986. Just seconds after the shuttle *Challenger* took off, it exploded. All seven

The giant orange tank and the two smaller white tanks are filled with fuel. They drop off the shuttle after their fuel is used up during blastoff. The shuttle then enters orbit. To land, it glides back to earth and lands much like an airplane.

astronauts were killed. They included mission specialist Judith Resnick and Christa MacAuliffe, the first teacher in space.

This was the second flight for Judith, who had flown on *Discovery's* first voyage in 1984. That earlier flight had several problems. Icicles formed on the outside of the shuttle. The ice could have damaged the ship. Judith used the shuttle's mechanical arm to chip all the ice away, and the shuttle returned safely.

Christa MacAuliffe was the first non-astronaut chosen for a space flight.

Christa MacAuliffe was excited about being the first teacher in space. She said,

"Imagine me teaching from space, all over the world, touching so many people's lives. That's a teacher's dream!"

In 2003, two other women were among the seven astronauts killed when the shuttle *Columbia* exploded.

Judith used a mechanical arm like this one to clean ice off Discovery so the shuttle could land safely.

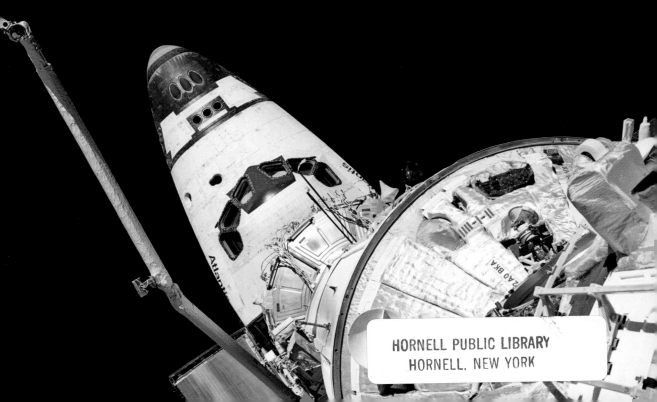

Since 1978, women have played more and more active roles in space exploration. They have been part of plenty of interesting "firsts." For example:

Medical doctor Mae Jemison helped the shuttle crew stay healthy in space.

- In 1984, Anna L. Fisher flew on the shuttle *Discovery* when her baby girl was only a year old.

- In 1992, Dr. Mae C. Jemison became the first African American woman in space.

- In 1996, Shannon Lucid lived on the Russian space station, *Mir*, for seven months. She was the first woman to spend that much time in space.

Here's Shannon floating on the Mir space station, where there is no gravity.

Since space flights began, almost 450 people have flown into space. Only about one-tenth of them have been women. That's mostly because some people had mistaken ideas about women when the space program began. Many people thought women weren't strong enough or smart enough for the job.

Women astronauts from Great Britain, Japan, India, France, and Canada have taken part in space missions.

The 40 women who have gone into space have proved them wrong. Now, almost one out of every four U.S. astronauts is a woman.

For today's girls who want to explore space, the sky is no limit—and neither are people's ideas about what girls can do!

Is Eileen Collins speaking to a future astronaut? You never know!

GLOSSARY

astrophysics the study of objects and events in space

capsule the small passenger area of a spacecraft

commander the person in charge, usually of a ship, airplane, or spacecraft

cosmonaut an astronaut in the Soviet and Russian space programs

gravity the force that holds us to the earth (in space, there is no gravity)

Mission Control the room back on Earth from which engineers help control space flights

mission specialist an astronaut trained for a specific job on a space flight, such as running the space shuttle's mechanical arm

orbit to go completely around something, usually a planet such as Earth

piloted drove or steered an aircraft or spacecraft

spacewalk go outside the spacecraft while in space; astronauts remain connected to the craft by special lines.

FIND OUT MORE

BOOKS

Mae Jemison: The First African American Woman in Space
by Magdalena Alagna
(Rosen Publishing, New York) 2003
Here's Dr. Mae Jemison's life story, including how she reached her goals.

Space for Women: A History of Women with the Right Stuff
by Pamela Freni
(Seven Locks Press, Santa Ana, CA) 2002
This is a great history of women who worked hard to become astronauts.

To Space and Back
by Sally Ride, with Susan Oakie
(HarperCollins, New York) 1986
Astronaut Sally Ride gives a photo-filled account of what it's really like to take a trip in the space shuttle.

Women of Space: Cool Careers on the Final Frontier
by Laura S. Woodmansee
(Collector's Guide, Burlington, Ontario) 2003
This book has plenty of information (including a CD-ROM) on careers in space exploration.

WEB SITES

Visit our home page for lots of links about astronauts and space travel: www.childsworld.com/links

Note to Parents, Teachers, and Librarians: We routinely check our Web links to make sure they're safe, active sites—so encourage your readers to check them out!

INDEX

N. B. GRACE has published a number of nonfiction books for children as well as novelizations for the Disney Channel. She lives in New York City, where she also writes plays and novels, creates collages, and participates in an active boxing program.